The Life of St. Fursey

What We Know; Why it Matters

MICHELLE P. BROWN

(Curator of Medieval and Illuminated Manuscripts, British Library)

Saturday 15th January, AD 2000

FURSEY OCCASIONAL PAPER NUMBER 1

First published in 2001 by

Fursey Pilgrims

3 Lancaster Gate, Bardney
Lincoln LN3 5BY

Reprinted 2003, 2007

ISBN 0 954477 30 8

Printed in England by

Postprint
Taverner House
East Harling, Norfolk

Introduction

The Fursey Pilgrims are an ecumenical group of Christians spanning a wide range of Christian traditions. We seek to encourage renewed interest in the life and times of St. Fursey – the first named, known missionary to Norfolk – and a deeper understanding of the spirituality of that era.

The Fursey Pilgrims came together in 1997, in the wake of the "Pilgrim's Way" initiative. That pilgrimage marked the 1,400th anniversary of the death of St. Columba and the arrival of St. Augustine. However, 1997 was also the 1,400th anniversary of the birth of St. Fursey, the Irish monk who worked in both East Anglia and northern France.

Among the activities of Fursey Pilgrims are the organisation of an annual pilgrimage to Burgh Castle, where Fursey's monastery is believed to have been located, on the first Saturday of October. There is also a celebration of Fursey's feast day on, or near to, 16th January. To mark the celebration in 2000, the Fursey Pilgrims invited Dr. Michelle Brown of the British Library to give an inaugural paper on St. Fursey. We are delighted to reproduce it here for wider circulation, as the first "Fursey Occasional Paper".

We are most grateful to the Bishop of Norwich for contributing a foreword to this paper, and for his kind assistance in making its publication possible.

Canon David Abraham

For further information on the Fursey Pilgrims,
telephone: 01603 402797
or visit our website at: www.furseypilgrims.co.uk

Foreword

One of the unexpected delights following my appointment as Bishop of Norwich was to discover St. Fursey. I have to admit that my knowledge of him prior to my arrival here was minimal. Discovering him, however, made me feel immediately at home. As a Cornishman exercising episcopal ministry in the Diocese of Truro, I thought that a move to East Anglia would take me well away from a land of Celtic saints. But those Celtic missionaries travelled quite as much in their own day as we do now, and the Christian tradition of East Anglia, looking back as it does to both St. Fursey and St. Felix, combines both the Celtic and Roman traditions – and, as far as we can tell, fairly harmoniously as well.

My enthronement progress around the diocese included Burgh Castle, and I was glad to return later in the year 2000 for the St. Fursey Pilgrimage there in October. Now the Fursey Pilgrims have been able to print Dr. Michelle Brown's stimulating inaugural lecture about St. Fursey. There is more to be known than I had imagined, and much more to be pondered. Perhaps East Anglia could yet provide a necessary counter to the way in which Celtic and Roman traditions of centuries past are seen as polarised rather than complementary. There is an ecumenical imperative in this research, and not just in the narrower church sense. The Christian tradition of those early centuries saw a unity between the created order and revealed Christian faith, a unity derived from Him in whom all things found their origin, even Jesus Christ our Lord.

+GRAHAM NORVIC:
May 2001

The Life of Saint Fursey

On Saturday 16th January, AD 1999, the feast day of St. Fursey, I experienced the great blessing and joy of joining the Fursey Pilgrims at the Church of St. Matthew, Thorpe Hamlet, Norwich, for a service in celebration of the life of Fursey. I had been invited to participate by giving a talk immediately after (or, as I prefer to consider it, as part of) that service on "Insular Art and Culture in the Time of St. Fursey". The following year I was back – this time accorded the honour of delivering the inaugural Fursey Lecture, in which I attempted to draw together what is known concerning his life and the development of his cult. The following represents the fruits of that quest.

It sometimes feels as if all paths lead to the British Library, at some time or another, if only as a symbol of the quest for knowledge. As one of the world's major repositories of some 3,000 years of recorded human endeavour and experience, it contains much of relevance to our common and individual journeys. The initial motive for the Fursey Pilgrims' enquiry was to discover the alleged source in a medieval illuminated manuscript for the depiction of St. Fursey in a nineteenth-century stained glass window in the church at Burgh Castle. The saint in question does not figure large in the corpus of Christian iconography. Among some 10,000 illuminated manuscripts preserved in the British Library collections there is only one known image relating to him: a pictorial representation of one of his visions that introduces a "readers' digest" summary of his *vita*, in a collection of saints' lives preserved in Royal MS 20.D.vi (f. 218), which was copied in NE France during the second half of the thirteenth century. This image depicts the vulnerable, naked human soul borne heavenwards by angels and protected by the shield of faith whilst demons fire deadly arrows at it (see back cover). This was not the image that the Fursey Pilgrims came in quest of. The window at Burgh Castle adopts a more tranquil, traditional form of iconography for the representation of saints. Here Fursey stands, clad in garb reminiscent of the Early Christian Mediterranean world, benignly contemplating the eternal and offering himself as the model of a static, conventional Christian hero. Further investigation revealed to us that the "lead" that had set the Furseymen onto their quest for a source for this pious Victorian image as "a manuscript in the British Museum", from which the British Library was about to move, was not entirely wrong. Having located our only recorded piece of Fursey iconography in said manuscript, my search of the rest of the book revealed that another of its miniatures (f. 17), depicting St. James the Great, had been taken as an appropriate model for the stoic, draped figure in his purple and blue robes. Naked, shivering souls and grimacing, blood-thirsty denizens of hell were evidently a little strong for the stomach of whoever designed the window glass. This person, who had evidently undertaken the research necessary to unearth one of the few surviving copies of material relating to Fursey, was looking for something closer to the similarly conventional "portraits" of the saint which are to be found in some other stained glass windows, such as those at Felixstowe and Gorleston. In the course of our deliberations some essential questions emerged: why is St. Fursey so comparatively little-known now, when it transpires that he was once an influential role model across much of NW Europe? What could be done to discover more about him and what he represented? Was there a valid purpose in so doing?

It so happened that my personal specialism is the culture of the Celts and Anglo-Saxons, so I had already encountered St. Fursey, and the fires of mutual enthusiasm were immediately kindled. Intermittently, over the next fourteen months or so, we had occasion to discuss what we know about Fursey and why he is important to us. Following last year's talk, and with the encouragement and participation of the Fursey Pilgrims and of scholars such as John Mitchell, Richard Emms and Oliver Rackham, we came to the view that an annual "St. Fursey Lecture" would be of value. This is humbly offered as the first of these. There are other lecture series that deal with the history and culture of early medieval Britain, notably the Jarrow Lectures (held annually in the Church of St. Paul, Jarrow, which incorporates fabric from the late seventh-century churches in which Bede worshipped) and also the Brixworth Lectures and the Deerhurst Lectures. The focuses for these series have all been notable surviving examples of Anglo-Saxon church fabric and their contents have ranged widely over the period of the sixth to eleventh centuries and have not necessarily dealt with matters of Christian interest, then or now. Quite properly, for even an active preoccupation with such matters can only be served by lively enquiry into all aspects of the period or cultures in question. However, we hope that the Fursey Lectures will set out to do something a little different: to take as their overt contemporary focus and inspiration the ecumenical celebration of the Christian faith, and to contribute to a sense of eternal communion whereby the study of the past actively stimulates and interacts with the spiritual life of the present, thereby sowing the seeds of growth for the future.

Let us start by summarising what we actually know about St. Fursey, how we have obtained that knowledge and some of the questions which might fruitfully be explored through further research, before going on to ask what relevance, beyond purely academic historical enquiry and its considerable social import, such knowledge holds for us. There are those who question the value of "history" and who feel that it is an encumbrance which impedes the embracing of the "modern" and of the future (we have heard a lot of discussion along such lines around the abstract phenomenon of the "Millennium" celebrations), or who feel that it has a purely commercial entertainment or "heritage" value. I am not amongst them. Nor do I intend to embark here upon any philosophical justification of the study of history or its many intellectual approaches and methods. What I do feel it worth saying here is that "history" is not "truth". Its study always serves contemporary agendas, however conscious or subconscious, overt or clandestine, communal or personal. If it did not, it would perhaps be unworthy of study in a vacuum. Such agendas should be acknowledged and their premises tested against historical evidence. It is when they distort and subvert such evidence, rather than assimilating and learning from it, that they can become destructive and counter-productive. Marxist history, gender studies and other agenda-orientated approaches to history all enjoy academic respectability. There is no need to feel coy about perpetuating and promoting the concept of participative Christian history.

Fursey is the earliest of a number of Irish religious who are known to have participated in the revival of Christianity in Britain and on the Continent in the post-Roman period. Christianity had been introduced to Britain and NW Europe during the Roman occupation, or perhaps slightly earlier if credence is given to the journey of

Joseph of Arimathea to England. During the course of the fourth century it became the state religion, although paganism co-existed, and there is a great deal of scholarly debate concerning the extent to which it survived the collapse of the western Roman Empire during the fifth century and the settlement of parts of its former territory by the pagan Germanic peoples. Nevertheless, by the sixth century the majority of inhabitants of England were pagan. In 597 St. Augustine arrived in Canterbury at the court of King Ethelbert of Kent and his Christian Frankish queen, Bertha. In 563 the princely Irish monk, St. Columba, had established a key foundation on Iona as part of his *peregrinatio* (exile for Christ), whence missionary work amongst the Picts and the Anglo-Saxons of Northumbria was launched, with Aidan succeeding in the foundation of the daughter monastery of Lindisfarne around 635. Together, and sometimes in competition, the Roman and Celtic Christian traditions and their representatives worked to transform England into a Christian kingdom – or, more correctly, a parcel of kingdoms. During the first half of the seventh century one of the most successful of the Anglo-Saxon kingdoms was East Anglia. Ethelbert of Kent had insisted that his client, King Redwald of East Anglia, who may have been the focus of commemoration at the famous Sutton Hoo cemetery, be baptised. Evidence suggests that the monotheistic deity of Christianity was simply added to Redwald's pantheon. Redwald's son, Eorpwald, also accepted baptism at the behest of King Edwin of Northumbria, leading to the swift assasination of the former by the pagan Ricbert and the apostatization of the region. These initial ventures in conversion were evidently embroiled in the dynastic politics of the day and it is unlikely that they permeated society to any extent. Eorpwald's brother, Sigebert, who may or may not have been Redwald's natural son, spent part of this period of turmoil in exile in Gaul and it was here that he was educated in a Christian environment and probably gained a respect for the work of Celtic religious who had embarked upon *peregrinatio* to the Continent in the footsteps of St. Columbanus (died 615), founder of such influential monasteries as Luxeuil in Gaul, St. Gall in Switzerland and Bobbio in northern Italy. Sigebert succeeded to the East Anglian kingship in 631 and, before his death in battle against the pagan King Penda of Mercia sometime before 644, he had worked with St. Honorius, the fifth archbishop of Canterbury, who had been sent to England by Pope Gregory the Great, to launch a missionary enterprise in East

Anglia. The Burgundian bishop Felix (died 648) came from Canterbury to found his see at Dunwich on the Suffolk coast. With Sigebert's assistance he established a school for boys staffed by teachers from Canterbury.

Such was the situation when, around 633, an abbot from the West coast of Ireland, St. Fursey, along with followers including his brothers, saints Foillan and Ultan, arrived in East Anglia and were welcomed by Sigebert and given a site called "Cnobheresburg" – thought to be the Roman "Saxon shore" fort of Burgh Castle near Great Yarmouth – in which to establish religious communities. Thus Fursey became the earliest recorded Irish monastic leader to work in England. Irish sources indicate that he was born to noble parents in 597, probably on an island in Lough Corrib, Co. Galway. Raised partly in Co. Kerry, with its rich early Christian tradition, Fursey founded a monastery near Cong, Co. Galway, and spent a decade preaching in Ireland before vowing to spend his life as a pilgrim for Christ, partly to escape the multitude of those seeking to follow him. In preparation he withdrew as a hermit to a remote island off of the west of Ireland before setting out on the voluntary exile that led him to the alien territory and landscape of East Anglia. The Frankish background of Sigebert and Felix would have ensured that the Celtic monastic tradition was familiar and venerable to them, if only by reputation, and must have contributed to the ready welcome accorded to the Irish band of pilgrims. The liturgical and jurisdictional controversies which were to lead to the Synod of Whitby in 664 were not yet an issue, and the representatives of both Roman and Celtic traditions appear to have worked together for the common cause of conversion. For a decade Fursey and his companions ministered to the people of Norfolk (who were perhaps even less prepared for their activities than those of Suffolk, the heartland of the kingdom). According to Bede the keys to Fursey's success were example and instruction, for people were "inspired by the example of his goodness and the effectiveness of his teaching, many unbelievers were drawn to Christ, and those who already believed were drawn to greater love and faith in him" (*Historia Ecclesiastica*, III.19). The reference to those who already believed is, in itself, intriguing and suggests that the situation was perhaps not as clear cut as it has been presented. The name "Fursey" or "Fursa" means virtue in Gaelic and, along with saints Columba,

Aidan and Cuthbert, he is used by Bede to exemplify the virtues of the Celtic tradition, whilst censuring its irregularities and potential separatism.

Fursey once again sought to escape his own success, feeling compelled to relinquish worldly concerns in favour of his spiritual journey. Another year of withdrawal and manual labour as a hermit, joining his brother Ultan in his hermitage, preceded his departure, around 644, for the Continent. He was concerned at the growing political instability and warfare and expressed the intention of undertaking a pilgrimage to Rome, where he would spend his life in prayer, leaving Cnobheresburg in the care of his brothers, who later followed him to Gaul. Its brethren were also active elsewhere in England, such as Dicuil, who established a hermitage at Bosham in the pagan territory of the South Saxons. The Christian rulers of East Anglia were defeated by the pagan King Penda. Sigebert had withdrawn to the monastic life, but sometime before 644 he was unwillingly brought back to lead his people into battle against the pagan Penda of Mercia. Refusing to carry arms in favour of a pilgrim's staff, he was killed along with his successor, King Egric. The foundations of Christianity in the region had been well-built, however, and Burgh was endowed with "finer buildings and gifts" by King Anna, Egric's successor, who was also killed by Penda in 654. It seems that Burgh was destroyed at this time but was refounded later in the century and continued in existence until the Viking incursions of the ninth century. Meanwhile, Fursey was highly active in the North of France, where he founded a monastery at Lagny-sur-Marne, East of Paris. The patronage and grant of the land on which to do so came from the Merovingian king and from Erchinoald, mayor of Neustria, whose household also included an attractive and competent English slave-girl, Bathild. She was to become the wife of the Merovingian King Clovis II, regent of Gaul, advocate of the abolition of slavery, founder of the monasteries of Corbie and Chelles, and a saint in her own right (despite probably erroneous accusations of political assassination). The area into which Fursey had ventured, the northern corner of France, had already been exposed to the Irish monastic tradition in the early seventh century through the work of Columbanus' follower, Valery of Leucone, and of the Irish (or perhaps British) Caidoc and Fricor and their disciple, Riquier. Yet it was Fursey's work which ensured the longer term effectiveness of the Irish mission in this area, and into Flanders where his brothers were subsequently active. He died around 649–650 at Mézerolles, whilst on a journey back to England, and was buried at Péronne, one of Earconwald's estates on which the latter was constructing a church. Fursey's body was placed in the porch (perhaps such a function inspired open porches, such as that at Monkwearmouth, which was built in 674–5 by Gaulish masons) and 27 days later was found to be incorrupt, the visible sign of sanctity, before being buried near the altar. A special chapel to the East of the altar was completed four years later and became the focus of his cult and a place of pilgrimage. Under his brothers and their successors it became such a magnet for Irish pilgrims that the monastery on the site was known as *peronna scottorum*. It retained its links with Ireland and England and may have been an important gateway to the two-way intellectual traffic between these areas and the Continent. Certainly works by the southern English scholar Aldhelm were being requested by Abbot Cellan in the eighth century. In 654 Fursey's relics were translated to said chapel and were displayed in a house-shaped shrine made by St. Eloi, bishop of Noyon, advisor to Queen Bathild and patron saint of metalworkers. Eloi received many important commissions for liturgical metalwork, no doubt encouraged by his reputation for making a little gold go a long way. This would indicate that the early shrine was probably a large version of the distinctive Celtic house-shaped reliquaries, of which a number of early examples survive (such as the Monymusk Reliquary and those now in Bologna and Siena). The importance of the cult was still attested by 1056, when the relics were once again translated (this process is similar to that which accompanied the growth of the cults of other leading saints, such as St. Cuthbert). Most of the relics remained intact until the French Revolution, and a head reliquary remained until the late nineteenth century. The inclusion of his feast day, 16th January, in many Irish, French and English calendars (including those of Canterbury, which claimed head-relics), bears witness to the popularity of his cult during the Middle Ages. He still figures in Irish and Continental devotions, but had become rather neglected in England, the focus of some of his most important work, until the recent revival of interest stimulated by the Fursey Pilgrims.

Fursey is attributed with many miracles during his lifetime, as well as those posthumously associated with his cult. These consist of miracles of healing (his staff and wells connected with him being attributed, in Celtic fashion, with similar powers by association) of the body (even extending to the raising from the dead of the young son of a Frankish duke, Haimon, in an episode consciously reminiscent of Jairus' daughter) and of immorality of spirit. He is not the righteous, hellfire cursing sort of saint. Rather, his miracle stories are characterised by charity and a sense of compassion which often led him to extend mercy to those who had done him wrong when they subsequently repented. He is also ascribed an interest in learning and is accredited with the composition of a lorica, or breastplate – a distinctive form of early Celtic prayer in which parts of the body are enumerated as part of a request that they be defended by the Lord from sin and are imbued with virtues. This has recently been translated, as follows:

> The arms of God be around my shoulders,
> The touch of the Holy Spirit upon my head,
> The sign of Christ's cross upon my forehead,
> The sound of the Holy Spirit in my ears,
> The fragrance of the Holy Spirit in my nostrils,
> The vision of heaven's company in my eyes
> The conversation of heaven's company on my lips,
> The work of God's church in my hands,
> The service of God and the neighbour in my feet,
> A home for God in my heart,
> And to God, the Father of all, my entire being.
> Amen.

Its use reminds us of the shield of faith in the later manuscript image.

One of his most influential contributions to the devotional genre was, however, his role as a visionary. During periods of illness he was visited by visions. The most distinctive of these was a journey in the company of angels in which, having been carried to a great height, he was able to see the delights of the blessed and the torments of the damned. At least, this is how they became enshrined in the medieval mind, culminating in Dante's *Paradisio* and *Inferno*. Fursey's vision is in some ways a subtler thing, in that he saw purifying fires representing falsehood, covetousness, discord and cruelty. All souls needed to be cleansed by these fires, but only if they had kindled them and to the measure by which they had done so, as a means of atonement. The prospect of such atonement is at variance with the theological concept of "saved" and "damned". Nonetheless, the physical assaults and slanders of demons figure vividly in Fursey's otherworld and became a powerful image.

Such then, with some additional detail of miracles, sayings and visions, is the extent of our knowledge of St. Fursey. How do we know even this much, and what are the nature and purpose of the sources? One of the most important written records is that embedded in *The History of the English Church and People*, or *Historia Ecclesiastica*, composed by the scholarly monk Bede at Jarrow and completed in 731. Here Bede gives us a thumbnail sketch of the saint's life, extrapolated from a "little book on his life" which the historian is at pains to acknowledge, or footnote, as his primary source. Thus a *vita* was in circulation by 730. Bede uses the Fursey episode as part of the third book of his work (Bk III, ch. 19), which deals with the processes by which the various Anglo-Saxon kingdoms were converted. These are characterised by the combined efforts of missionaries of both "Roman" and "Celtic" background, who work together, or rather in parallel, for the common cause. Their efforts are then generally undermined by pagan offensives leading to apostatization usually followed by the triumph of the Christian faith owing to the firm foundations already laid. This book also deals with the controversies that arose because of variant practices between the two clerical traditions, culminating in the Synod of Whitby, and the polarised or reconciliatory stances adopted by various of their members. Book IV goes on to examine the more stable, organised ecclesiastical structure built upon the early foundations in the wake of reconciliation of differences. Fursey is therefore an ideal illustration for Bede's didactic purposes: an ideal representative of the strengths of the Celtic tradition who interacted collaboratively with the Roman mission in England and the Church in Gaul, and who saw Rome as the earthly goal of his *peregrinatio* heavenwards. His visions were also recognised by Bede for the value of their strong didactic imagery, as symbolic word-pictures of the sort beloved by the

Insular mind. Bede's work was a medieval best-seller and was thereby instrumental in preserving Fursey's memory for posterity.

This early core of the "Life of Fursey", which has become known as the *Vita Prima Fursei* and which is ascribed a date of composition in the seventh century soon after his death, along with the Bedan extrapolation, was built upon subsequently. During the early ninth century it gave rise to a text known as the "Virtues of Fursey" *(Virtutes Fursei)* which relate his miracles. There are many manuscripts which contain these Latin texts. Some contain only the *Vita*, some add the *Virtutes* and others add the *Additamentum Nivialense de Fuilano*, a continuation added at the daughter house of Nivelles in the seventh century. The texts were published in the seventeenth century by the Bollandists and a Latin edition based on all the manuscript sources was edited by Krusch in *Monumenta Germaniae Historica*. There is no published English translation, save for the material contained in Bede's History. (This is something that the Fursey Pilgrims might care to commission.) The earliest extant copy of the *Vita Prima* is, to my best of my knowledge, contained in B.L., Harley MS 5041, ff. 79–100 (CLA 2.202 a and b). This was copied in northern France in the eighth century (probably mid-century) and also contains other works relating to the ascetic tradition by Isidore of Seville and others. The "Life" is by a different hand to the rest of the book, and the way in which this part is assembled (its codicology) differs, but it appears to have been intended to form part of the same book. Both hands are undoubtedly working in Gaul, but that responsible for the "Life" exhibits a mixed background, combining features of Merovingian script, Beneventan letter forms perhaps pointing to the influence of Italian script models, and distinctive abbreviations and manner of preparing the gatherings to receive writing which point to Insular influence. The one decorated initial, in the other part of the book, has been compared to work from Bathild's foundation of Corbie. Given this mixture of features it is not unreasonable to suggest that the volume was copied in the part of northern France in which Fursey had worked a century beforehand. Other early copies include B.L., Egerton MS 2797, ff. 87v-109, from tenth-century Hainault or environs, where it is part of a collection of saints' lives.

A second Latin version of the "Life of Fursey", the *Vita Secunda*, was composed on the Continent during the eleventh to twelfth centuries. It is attributed to two monks, Serlo and Rotbertus, and has a prefatory epistle by Arnulf, Abbot of Lagny, who died in 1106. Associated are two hymns in honour of St. Fursey ("Laudes almi confessoris" and "Laeta plaude Hibernia"). The Latin versions of the "Life" were also extrapolated from in later medieval compendia of legends of saints. An anonymous French translation appears in B.L., Royal MS 20.D.vi, the northern French manuscript of the second half of the thirteenth-century, which contains the miniatures with which this account began. This is part of a family of texts, distinct from the *Legenda Aurea*, which has been discussed by M. Paul Meyer (*Hist. Lit. de la France*, 33, 1906, p. 411). No single Latin source for these lives occurs, and it is likely that they were being compiled from a variety of earlier sources, such as the earlier lives of Fursey already discussed.

A vernacular Irish version of the early "Life" was also made, featuring the account of the visions that particularly captured the Celtic imagination and became influential in Irish literature. This is preserved in Brussels, Bibl. Royale, MS 2324–40, ff. 158–160, and Dublin, Royal Irish Academy, MS A.iv.I (Stowe 9), pp. 165–174.

Other corroborative details are found in historical sources. The *Annales Laubienses* refer to his pilgrimage to Gaul, and to the arrival of Foillan and Ultan in 649. Documents from the early Irish monastery of Tallaght also contain references to his work in Ireland and to some of his acts and sayings (such as his comparison of the anvil he metaphorically carried upon his back as "the perseverance in holiness") and the *Annals of Ulster* record his death under 649. Other hagiographical and historical texts also relate to his brothers and other followers.

Place-name evidence should also be considered. It has been assumed that Burgh Castle is the site of Fursey's foundation, but this is perhaps worth exploring, for there are other possible sites for the fortification which Bede tells us was donated by Sigebert, such as Caistor-on-Sea nearby. Bede tells us that "this monastery was pleasantly situated in some woods close to the sea, within the area of a fortification that the English call Cnobheresburg, meaning Cnobhere's Town". Burgh Castle is first called "Burch" in Domesday Book. As a place-name element "burh" can mean "fortification", "town" or "small hill or mound". The early name-form in Bede indicates a settlement which belonged to someone named Cnobhere or Cnofhere in the early Anglo-Saxon period. The place-name scholar Margaret Gelling has established that the generic term "burh" was well represented by 730. It could denote anything from a prehistoric fort to a manor house, coming to mean "town" later in the Anglo-Saxon period (as with Bury St. Edmunds) when Alfred and his successors were establishing fortified towns as part of their reconquest of the Danelaw. Burgh Castle is one of the rare instances, along with Burgh by Sands in Cumbria, of it referring to a Roman fort (Burgh Castle was called Garianno in the Roman period). The Latin for fort, "castrum", is more commonly adapted to Old English "Cæster", or "Caistor". This is the name that one might have expected to be applied to Burgh Castle, but if the Roman fort there had been appropriated by an early Englishman and had become known by an English name, this would explain the later contraction from Cnobheresburg to Burgh. Place-name evidence would therefore tend to support its identification as the site of Fursey's monastery. Bede also tells us that it was in woodland by the sea. The great Roman port which once stood adjacent to the site is now silted up and centuries of farming have altered the landscape, but woods and water remain as vestiges of the early landscape. The site has not been fully excavated, but archaeological explorations of the site in 1958–61 are said to have revealed some Anglo-Saxon artefacts and traces of wattle and daub buildings, including what was tentatively proposed as a beehive hut of Celtic type. The weight of evidence therefore points to Burgh Castle as the likely site. The nearby church retains late Anglo-Saxon fabric but, curiously, does not occupy the fortified site. Perhaps traces of the early churches had disappeared by this time and only the recollection of sanctity remained, or perhaps the later church was seen as adjacent to the early site.

There are several cases in which Germanic kings granted the sites of Roman fortifications to early missionaries, notably Bradwell-on-Sea and Dover. What remained of the walls – and there are considerable remains still standing at Burgh – would have offered protection and building materials, and the cultural resonance would have accorded with the wish of such rulers to present themselves as the natural successors or heirs of Rome by promoting a Christian, literate culture. Such foundations would have been visible symbols of "romanitas", even if staffed by Celtic monks. The "Virtues of Fursey" relates that Fursey and his companions built monasteries and churches for monks and nuns on the land they received in East Anglia, and implies that they became a magnet for the infirm. Bede informs us that King Anna donated finer buildings, and so we may envision a thriving centre of activity with a mixed population and a mission of outreach. This would accord with a prominent strand of Celtic monasticism in which such centres functioned virtually as extended families (or "derbfine", as they are known in Irish) dedicated to the service of the Lord rather than to worldly agendas. It should be considered, however, that the passage in the "Virtues" reflects not so much East Anglian reality as supplying a context for double monasteries for monks and nuns, which were popular in early Christian Gaul. Given the nature of relations between the regions it is not unlikely, however, that such traditions were inter-related. Other double monasteries in the Celtic tradition are well-attested in Anglo-Saxon England, notably Hild's Whitby.

This then is the nature of the evidence for the person and the site. What, other than respect and nostalgia, might prompt an ecumenical Christian heading into the twenty-first century of the Christian era to revive interest in them? Celtic spirituality is undergoing something of a general revival. In the face of the relentless pace of society, its rampant materialism and its monolithic corporate identities and regulation, a tradition which strikes a resonance concerning the balance between active and contemplative, of the place of the individual within the communal, of "green" issues, approaches to conflict and symbolism, which underpins so much of our contemporary approach to communications, is bound to be attractive. Yet there is something of a danger of using the "Celtic" label as a cover for laxity of approach and as a reaction against structure, resulting in a "cuddly Celtic Christianity" which bears little relationship to the tradition it purports to perpetuate. For example, anyone tempted to use the "freedom" afforded by the Celtic tradition as an argument against discipline and structure should first acquaint themselves with the Rule of Columbanus and the many Irish Penitentials.

One of the major points of interest of the Fursey material for a modern Christian audience is the example it offers of constructive collaboration between representatives of different traditions of churchmanship in order to further their common Christian mission. The ecumenical implications of this are immediately apparent. Nonetheless, the converse of this has been a tendency among historians and Christian commentators to over-emphasise the extent of the divergence between the early Celtic and Roman traditions and the period of time for which they were an issue. Most members of the early medieval church in the Celtic regions would have been appalled at the claims of separatism and independence which are laid at their door. They are more likely to have seen themselves as working for a universal Christian communion which was ecumenical in that it was able to tolerate and fuse strengths from very different cultural traditions.

The *peregrinatio*, or voluntary exile for Christ, is a phenomenon which also has something to offer the present. It should be understood against the background of secular Irish law, in which it represented the most severe level of deterrent, alongside capital punishment. To remove oneself, or to be expelled, from the social structures of kingship and kindred was to fall outside of any means of legal or economic support. You became, in effect, an outlaw, but were also freed of any attendant obligations, other than to the Lord, in the case of those religious who so chose. Such an option also freed one, in spiritual terms, from what early sources describe as one of the greatest of earthly sorrows: the attachment to loved ones and the fear and grief of separation in life or in death. Vanquishing such fears and recognising a more fundamental allegiance to God was part of the religious discipline and still has something to offer in terms of fostering the recognition that love can be sustained even when deprived of proximity and physical contact.

The course of Fursey's career is an interesting one, reminiscent of that of St. Cuthbert, in that he obeyed a call to share his faith with others through teaching, preaching and pastoral ministrations, but that he seems to have felt himself frequently a victim of his own success. This led him to withdraw to the seclusion and hardship of the eremitic retreat. Such periods were not an escape from the world, however, but times of questioning and purification before re-entering the fray with renewed vigour. The balance between active and contemplative modes and the recognition that there can be seasons for each is something which our "24-hour society" neglects at its peril. Steadfastness of purpose is, however, also a feature of Fursey's outlook. He conceived of a purpose and continued to work towards it. His pilgrimage to Rome as part of his quest for the heavenly kingdom remained a long-term goal. His arrival in East Anglia should perhaps be seen as part of this longer *peregrinatio* from the start and his subsequent departure for Gaul may have been less a recognition of the perilous times than of the appropriate timing for the next stage in the journey. Nonetheless, he always responded to the work which God and man revealed for him en route. His own self-determined goal on earth was never achieved. He never prayed at the sites graced by saints Peter and Paul, but this aim motivated and structured his journey and validated the work en route, assisted by prayer, meditation and study, as well as good works. For Fursey it was perhaps better to travel hopefully than to arrive, and the failure to attain the appointed earthly goal did not subtract from the journey towards the heavenly or spiritual home.

Finally, the virtues of Fursey illustrate, in a succinct and vivid form, the vital interaction of the processes of sin, conscience, acknowledged responsibility, atonement, compassion and forgiveness. None of these are strangers to Christianity in the 21st century, any more than they were in Fursey's time.

The Insular tradition placed a great emphasis upon the *communio sanctorum* (communion of saints). Liturgy incorporated it, commentaries dealt with it and images such as the "Temptation" in the *Book of Kells* and the evangelist miniatures in the *Book of Cerne* (which form part of a protracted meditation on its nature in prayerbook form) symbolically encapsulated it. Such communion weaves together time, space and all Creation in one body, with Christ as its head. As part of that shared communion, Fursey's journey still has a bearing on our own.

Bibliography

General and historical

H. Mayr-Harting, *The Coming of Christianity to Anglo-Saxon England* (London, 1972).

Dorothy Whitelock, "The Pre-Viking Age Church in East Anglia", *Anglo-Saxon England* 1 (1972), 1–22.

Margaret Gelling, "A Chronology for Suffolk Place-Names", in M. Carver, ed., *The Age of Sutton Hoo* (Woodbridge, 1992), pp. 53–64.

Jane Stevenson, "Christianity in Sixth- and Seventh-Century Southumbria", in Carver, *Age of Sutton Hoo*, pp. 175–184.

R. Ní Mheara, *In Search of Irish Saints* (Dublin, 1994).

L. Traube, *Perrona Scottorum…*, Sitgunsgb. K. Bayer. Akad. Wiss., philos-philol. Kl, 4 (Munich, 1900), pp, 469–538.

M. Stokes, *Three Months in the Forests of France: A Pilgrimage in Search of Vestiges of Irish Saints in France* (London, 1895).

S. Youngs, *The Work of Angels: Masterpieces of Celtic Metalwork, 6th–9th centuries AD* (London & Austin, 1989).

T. Joyce, *Celtic Christianity* (Maryknoll, NY, 1998).

F. E. Warren, "St. Fursey", *Proc. Suffolk Inst. Archaeol.* 16 (1918), 252–277.

L. H. Dahl, *The Roman Camp and the Irish Saint at Burgh Castle with Local History* (London, 1913).

N. Friart, *Histoire de St. Fursey…* (Lille, 1913).

W. H. Kirwan, "Some Celtic Missionary Saints – St. Fursey", *Irish Ecclesiastical Record*, 4th ser., 32 (1912), 170–187.

J. Hennig, "The Irish Background of St. Fursey", *Irish Ecclesiastical Record*, 5th ser., 77 (1952), 18–28.

Gruetzmacher, "Die Viten des heiligen Furseus", *Zeit. Kirchengesch.* 19 (1899), 190–196.

C. S. Boswell, *An Irish Precursor of Dante* (London, 1908), pp. 166–169.

Sources and editions

For a summary of the sources, see J. F. Kenney, *The Sources for the Early History of Ireland: Ecclesiastical* (Dublin, 1979), no. 296.

Bollandists, *Acta Sanctorum*, Jan. II (Antwerp, 1643), pp. 35–55; (Louvain, 1645), pp. 75 et seq., etc. (see Kenney).

B. Krusch, *"Vita virtutesque Fursei…"*, *Monumenta Germaniæ Historica, script. Rerum Merovingicarum, 4. Passiones vitaeque sanctorum*, pp. 423–451: 7, pp. 837–842 (Hanover, 1902, 1920).

Bede, *Ecclesiastical History of the English People*, transl. L. Shirley Price et al., Penguin Classics (revd edn, London, 1990), pp. 171–176.

B. Colgrave and R. A. B. Mynors, eds, *Historia Ecclesiastica Gentis Anglorum* (Oxford, 1979).

W. Stokes, ed. and transl., "Betha Fursa, the Life of Fursa", *Revue Celtique* 25 (1904), 385–404 (Irish text and English translation, based on Brussels, Royal Library, MS 2324).

P. Ó Riain, "Les Vies de saint Fursey: les Sources Irlandaises", *Revue du Nord* 68 (1986), 405–413.

T. Davila, *Historia y vida del admirabile…San Furseo* (Madrid, 1699).

CLA = E. A. Lowe, *Codices Latini Antiquiores* (11 vols and suppl., Oxford 1934–1972).